HE WHO
FINDS A
Wife

A Husbands Call To War

TORRANCE MACKINS JR.

"He who finds a wife finds a war worth fighting." "You're not just the husband—you're the front line." "Love leads. Prayer protects. A husband does both."

Contents

Introduction. The Battle Begins With You. 1

Chapter 1.   A Man After God's Heart. 5

Chapter 2.   The Husband as Priest and Protector 11

Chapter 3.   The Real Enemy. 18

Chapter 4.   Warring with Love and Sacrifice. 25

Chapter 5.   The Sword of the Spirit. 31

Chapter 6.   Guarding Her Mind and Emotions 38

Chapter 7.   Warring as One 45

Chapter 8.   Raising the Standard in the Home 52

Chapter 9.   Born to War, Called to Love 59

The Battle Begins With You

Why this fight matters—and why it starts with your heart.

This book is not a manual for perfect husbands. It's a call to warring husbands—men who are willing to fight for their marriages, their homes, and their wives with courage, conviction, and spiritual authority.

You were not made to drift through marriage. You were not created to survive fatherhood, endure leadership, or limp through your calling. You were made to stand. To cover. To protect. To lead.

But none of that matters if your own heart is still enslaved.

You can't fight for your wife's peace if your soul has no peace with God.

You can't lead her spiritually if you're still walking in darkness.

You can't build a godly home on a godless foundation.

Before this book calls you to war for your wife, it must call you to surrender to Jesus. Because all spiritual authority flows from relationship, not religion. You don't become a godly husband by trying harder. You become one by dying to yourself and living in Christ.

Why the Battle Is So Intense

Satan hates marriage. He always has.

From the beginning, he's tried to divide what God joined. And make no mistake—he's not just after your happiness. He's after your legacy. Your children. Your example. Your potential. Your unity. He knows a godly marriage can shift generations.

But you are not helpless. You are not weak. You are not stuck.

Through Christ, you've been given everything you need to war well:

- The Word of God
- The Spirit of God
- The authority of a surrendered life

But that authority begins with this question: Have you given your life to Jesus?

If You're Not Saved, Everything Else Falls Apart

You can be a great provider. You can be loyal and strong. But without Christ, you're spiritually dead. You're still in your sin. You may build a decent house—but it won't stand when the storm comes.

> "Unless the Lord builds the house, the builders labor in vain." (Psalm 127:1)

This book will give you tools. But only Jesus gives you a new heart.

This book may give you strategy. But only Jesus gives you salvation.

And without Him, you're fighting a battle you're not equipped to win.

So before you read another chapter, here's the most important question I could ever ask you:

Have You Given Your Life to Jesus Christ?

Not religion. Not church attendance. Not belief in God generally.

But full surrender. Repentance. Trusting that Jesus died for your sins, rose from the dead, and is now Lord over your life.

He doesn't want a better version of you—He wants you, surrendered and made new.

"If anyone is in Christ, he is a new creation." (2 Corinthians 5:17)

"Everyone who calls on the name of the Lord will be saved." (Romans 10:13)

▌ If You're Ready, Pray This:

"Jesus, I need You. I confess I'm a sinner and I can't save myself.

I believe You died for me. I believe You rose from the grave.

I ask You to forgive me, cleanse me, and make me new.

I give You my heart. I give You my life.

Be my Savior. Be my Lord. Be my foundation.

Fill me with Your Spirit. Teach me how to love, lead, and live like You.

From this day forward, I belong to You.

In Jesus' name, amen."

If you prayed that prayer, welcome to the fight—with power. You are now forgiven. Adopted. Empowered. Covered in grace. And ready to lead from the place of surrender.

Let's begin the journey of warring for your wife—not with pride, but with passion.

Not in your strength, but in His.

Let the battle begin.

CHAPTER 1

A Man After God's Heart

Before you fight for her, you must belong fully to Him.

Before you ever lead your wife into the heart of God, you must live there yourself. The war for your marriage doesn't start in the home—it starts in the hidden place. And your greatest strength as a husband is not in your ability to provide or protect. It's in your willingness to pursue the presence of God.

Many men want to lead well, love deeply, and war courageously. But few understand that everything flows from the condition of their heart before God.

You can't give what you haven't received. You can't cover her spiritually if your own spirit is uncovered. You can't protect your house from darkness if your private world is filled with compromise.

So before you draw your sword, pick up your harp.

David: The Shepherd-Warrior

When God rejected Saul as king, He didn't go looking for a taller man, a better warrior, or someone with more credentials. He looked for a heart.

> "The Lord has sought out a man after His own heart and appointed him ruler of His people." (1 Samuel 13:14)

That man was David.

Before he was ever a king or a warrior, David was a worshiper. In the fields, alone with sheep and silence, he learned how to chase after God. He cultivated a heart of intimacy, repentance, and faith. He wrote songs in obscurity. He fought off lions and bears when no one was watching. He built a history with God that would become his greatest weapon in every battle to come.

When David faced Goliath, it wasn't armor or strategy that gave him confidence—it was the God he had come to know in secret.

Men often want to be warriors in public, but they haven't learned to be worshipers in private.

David's victories didn't start on the battlefield. They started in the pasture.

What Does It Mean to Be After God's Heart?

To be "after God's heart" means to chase what God loves. It means you're not living for applause, but alignment. It means you're willing to lay down your pride, your preferences, and your need to be in control because you're more obsessed with God's presence than your own power.

David wasn't perfect. He sinned grievously. He made massive mistakes. But he kept coming back to the feet of God. That's what set him apart. His sin didn't define him—his repentance did.

Men, God isn't looking for perfection. He's looking for pursuit.

The Private Battle Prepares You for the Public One

Before you can protect her peace, you must guard your own mind.

Before you can intercede for her future, you must submit your own plans to God.

Before you can carry her burdens, you must be willing to be carried by Christ.

Your spiritual authority in the home is directly tied to your spiritual alignment with heaven.

You don't get authority just because you're a man. You walk in authority when you live submitted to the King.

Modern Distractions to a God-Chasing Heart

In today's world, the average man is pulled in every direction:

- Hustling for provision
- Numbing stress with entertainment
- Silencing conviction with busyness
- Avoiding spiritual leadership out of fear or insecurity

The result? A passive man with a distracted heart and a vulnerable home.

Here's the truth: if you don't lead your heart, the world will.

Practical Ways to Become a Man After God's Heart

1. Prioritize Presence Over Productivity
   - Start your day with worship, not a to-do list.
   - Even 15 minutes in prayer realigns your soul.

2. Read the Word to Know Him, Not Just Learn Facts
   - Don't study the Bible just to be right—read it to be close.

3. Repent Quickly and Often
   - Humility is attractive to heaven.
   - Keep short accounts with God and your wife.

4. Worship When No One Is Watching
   - Create a secret history with God that hell can't duplicate.

5. Fast From Distraction
    ○   Turn off what dulls your desire for God.
    ○   What feeds your flesh will always starve your spirit.

Personal Reflection Questions

- Have I made intimacy with God a daily priority, or a backup plan?
- What areas of my heart have I withheld from God's rule?
- Am I building strength in the hidden place—or relying on my natural ability to lead?
- What would change in my marriage if I fully surrendered to God?

Devotional Prayer: A Warrior's Heart

Father,

I don't want to lead without You. I don't want to fight without You. I don't want to win in life and lose in the secret place. Make me a man after Your heart. Strip away every idol, every distraction, every excuse. Teach me to worship when no one is watching. Teach me to hunger for Your presence more than I hunger for success or control.

Forgive me for every time I tried to lead my wife without first listening to You.

Forgive me for building platforms without altars.

Fill me with Your Spirit.

Break me where I need to be broken.

Strengthen what's been passive in me.

Make me dangerous to the enemy—not because I'm strong, but because I'm Yours.

Today, I take up my harp before I pick up my sword.

Shape me in the quiet place, so I can stand in the battle.

Let my heart beat in rhythm with Yours.

In Jesus' name,

Amen.

CHAPTER 2

The Husband as Priest and Protector

Before you defend her body, defend her spirit.

A man's greatest battles aren't fought with fists—they're fought in prayer. The most dangerous husband is not the loudest man in the room, or the one who's physically strong. It's the man who wakes up early, bends low in humility, and lifts up his wife's name in intercession.

He doesn't need applause. He doesn't need a platform. He just needs to know his role: priest and protector.

Before you ever war for your wife with your hands, you war for her with your heart. You are not just her partner—you are her spiritual covering.

Job: The Forgotten Warrior of Intercession

Job may not be the first name you think of when it comes to husbands who war for their families, but look closer.

> "Early in the morning, he would sacrifice a burnt offering for each of them, thinking, 'Perhaps my children have sinned and cursed God in their hearts.' This was Job's regular custom." (Job 1:5)

Job didn't wait until disaster struck to pray. He didn't need a crisis to activate his faith. He covered his family just in case. He rose early. He interceded. He acted like a priest.

And when all hell broke loose in Job's life, heaven had already heard his name.

You may never stand on a stage or preach a sermon—but you can cover your household in prayer like Job. You can build an altar where your family is safe from what the eye can't see.

That's what spiritual protection looks like.

The Role of a Priest in the Home

In the Old Testament, the priest had four responsibilities:

1. Offer sacrifices
2. Intercede on behalf of the people
3. Maintain holiness in the tabernacle
4. Speak God's blessing

Today, as a husband, that role hasn't changed—just the sacrifice. You don't bring lambs to the altar. You bring your life. You lay down your time, your comfort, and your pride.

You don't pray around your wife. You pray over her.

You don't wait for her to initiate spiritual conversations. You lead them.

You don't rely on your pastor to cover your home. You are the priest God has assigned to it.

The Two Front Lines of Spiritual Protection

1.
Intercession

The enemy doesn't wait for an invitation—he looks for an opening. He attacks when you're distracted, passive, or assuming everything is fine.

- Your wife might look strong—but is her heart weary?
- She might be smiling—but is her mind under assault?

You can't afford to assume she's okay. You must pray in advance. Cover her thoughts, her emotions, her identity, her purpose.

Pray protection.
Pray deliverance.
Pray restoration.
Pray healing.

Every husband must have a war room—even if it's the driver's seat of your car or the bathroom floor at 6 a.m.

2.
Discernment

The priest wasn't just a man of prayer. He was a man of awareness.

Discernment isn't suspicion—it's sensitivity to the Holy Spirit.

- What has shifted in the atmosphere of your home?
- Are arguments increasing?
- Is peace harder to find?
- Is your wife more withdrawn, anxious, or irritable?

Don't criticize her condition—confront the spirit behind it.

Sometimes what looks like mood swings is actually spiritual oppression. What seems like disrespect is actually fear. What feels like distance is often emotional exhaustion.

A husband who protects spiritually doesn't just fix the surface. He digs to the root and covers it in prayer.

What Opens the Door to Attack in the Home?

- Compromise (tolerating sin or spiritual apathy)
- Neglect (letting your marriage run on autopilot)
- Disunity (allowing offense or bitterness to remain)
- Busyness (no margin for God, no margin for each other)

The devil loves tired, distracted men. They're easier to bypass.

But when a husband stands alert, filled with the Spirit, rooted in the Word—he becomes a wall that darkness cannot penetrate.

How to Cover Her Daily

1. Pray Out Loud Over Her
   - Before she leaves the house, speak a blessing.
   - At night, place your hand on her and ask God to refresh her soul.

2. Anoint Your Home
   - Use oil as a symbol. Pray over doorposts, windows, rooms.
   - Declare your home as a place where no demonic influence has access.

3. Set the Tone Spiritually
   - Turn on worship music.
   - Read Scripture together.
   - Lead conversations about what God is doing in your lives.

4. Fast for Breakthrough
   - If your wife is facing a battle, fast one day a week.
   - Show her you're not just "thinking of her"—you're warring for her.

Reflection Questions

- Am I waiting for my wife to initiate spiritual leadership?
- Have I allowed busyness or distraction to dull my discernment?
- What spiritual threats have I ignored that may be affecting my wife or children?
- Have I taken authority over my home in prayer?

Devotional Prayer: The Watchman's Cry

Father,

Today, I step fully into my role as priest and protector of my home. I refuse to live passively while the enemy prowls. I reject laziness, distraction, and fear. Make me alert in the Spirit. Give me discernment beyond what I can see with my eyes. Teach me to intercede before the battle ever reaches my front door.

I plead the blood of Jesus over my wife.

I cover her heart, her mind, her emotions, and her future.

No weapon formed against her shall prosper.

No voice of accusation shall define her.

No darkness shall dwell where Your light is present.

Let my prayers be a hedge.

Let my home be a sanctuary.

Let my leadership reflect the authority of heaven.

I take up my post as a watchman today.

Not in fear—but in faith.

Not in pride—but in obedience.

Not in silence—but with spiritual fire.

In the name of Jesus,

Amen.

CHAPTER 3

The Real Enemy

⊩ Your wife is not your opponent—hell is.

Conflict is inevitable in marriage. But how you see the conflict will determine whether you destroy each other—or the devil's plan. Far too many husbands are fighting with their wives when they should be fighting for them. And behind every lingering offense, emotional shutdown, or communication breakdown is a spiritual enemy who thrives on your confusion.

Satan's strategy is simple: distraction, division, and deception. If he can turn your attention away from him and aim it at her, he's already won.

> "For we do not wrestle against flesh and blood, but against principalities… against spiritual forces of evil in the heavenly realms." (Ephesians 6:12)

Your wife is not the enemy. She is your ally. The real enemy is subtle, patient, and persistent. He doesn't always attack with catastrophe. Sometimes he just whispers until doubt and distance take root.

Adam & Eve: The Serpent in the Garden

Genesis 3 tells the tragic story of the fall. But look carefully—it's not just a story about disobedience. It's about spiritual passivity.

> "She also gave some to her husband, who was with her, and he ate it." (Genesis 3:6)

Adam was with her. He wasn't off working. He wasn't unaware. He was silent. The serpent lied, twisted God's word, seduced Eve with empty promises—and Adam said nothing. He didn't confront the lie. He didn't cover his wife. He allowed deception to go unchecked.

That silence cost them everything.

The first marriage was fractured not because of hatred or abuse—but because the man refused to identify and confront the real enemy.

Satan still slithers into homes today:

- Through offense left unresolved
- Through isolation masked as "space"
- Through temptation dressed as opportunity
- Through exhaustion that numbs spiritual sensitivity

You must open your eyes. Because what you don't fight will fester.

The Enemy's Tactics in Marriage

1. Division
   - The enemy knows a house divided cannot stand (Mark 3:25).
   - He doesn't need to destroy your love—just break your agreement.

2. Assumption
   - When communication breaks down, the devil fills in the blanks with suspicion and accusation.

3. Emotional Distortion
   - He warps what you hear: "She's disrespecting you."
   - He twists what she feels: "He doesn't care about you."

4. Rehearsing Offense
   - Instead of remembering God's Word, you rehearse what they said last week.
   - Offense becomes a false narrative the enemy loves to write.

How to Identify Spiritual Attack

Sometimes what seems like a "bad mood" or "just a rough season" is actually an assignment from hell. Here's how you recognize it:

- Patterns
  Does the same issue keep surfacing, no matter how often it's addressed?

- Sudden emotional shifts
  Is she suddenly anxious, hopeless, or unusually withdrawn?

- Escalation without cause
  Do small conversations suddenly turn into big arguments?

- Spiritual dryness
  Is there a fog over your prayer life? A resistance to worship or intimacy?

Discernment asks, What's influencing this? not just What's happening?

Jesus and Peter: Recognizing the Voice Behind the Voice

In Matthew 16, Peter tells Jesus, "You will never go to the cross." Jesus doesn't coddle Peter. He recognizes the spirit behind the sentiment.

> "Get behind Me, Satan! You are a stumbling block to Me." (Matthew 16:23)

Jesus didn't attack Peter's person—He addressed the source.

That's how you must learn to war. Not by fighting her feelings—but by confronting the spiritual force behind them.

Is the enemy using fear to speak through her?

Is insecurity clouding what she's trying to communicate?

Is shame shutting down her openness?

As a husband, your job isn't to win the argument. It's to lead through the confusion with spiritual clarity.

What to Do When You Sense an Attack

1. Pause the argument—pray instead.
   - Don't keep shouting in the flesh. Pause and say, "Let's pray right now."
   - It may feel awkward—but it will shut the door on the enemy.

2. Take spiritual authority out loud.
   - Declare, "This house belongs to Jesus. Every spirit of confusion or division must leave in His name."
   - The devil can't read minds, but he trembles when you speak with faith.

3. Ask heaven, not your ego, what's happening.
   - Holy Spirit, show me what's behind this tension. Where's the open door?

4. Call it what it is.
   - If bitterness is growing, name it.
   - If pride is fueling the division, confess it.
   - If shame is manipulating her view of herself, speak God's truth over her.

Reflection Questions

- Have I mistaken my wife's wounds for warfare instead of wounding?
- Am I quick to assume the worst—or slow to seek spiritual truth?
- What lies have I let live in my marriage by refusing to confront them?
- Is there a spiritual stronghold operating in my home that I've ignored?

Devotional Prayer: Eyes to See the Enemy

Father,

Open my eyes. Help me see the real battle. Forgive me for every time I fought with my wife instead of fighting for her. Teach me to recognize the schemes of the enemy. Give me discernment beyond my emotions. Give me patience in conflict, compassion in misunderstanding, and spiritual boldness when darkness tries to invade my home.

I take back authority today.

I silence every lie.

I break every assignment of division, offense, and fear.

I declare that my marriage is not up for negotiation.

Teach me to war in the Spirit—quick to pray, slow to accuse, strong in truth, and humble in love.

I will no longer be passive in the battle.

I will no longer mistake her pain as an attack on me.

Make me a man who sees clearly and wars accordingly.

In Jesus' name,

Amen.

CHAPTER 4

Warring with Love and Sacrifice

You win her heart through surrender, not control.

Strength isn't shown by how loud you are in conflict. True strength is seen in how low you're willing to go in love. The world tells men to fight for dominance. God calls husbands to fight through dying.

The model isn't cultural masculinity—it's Calvary.

> "Husbands, love your wives, just as Christ loved the church and gave Himself up for her."
>
> (Ephesians 5:25)

This isn't poetic language. It's a mandate. You are to love her in a way that bleeds. In a way that costs. In a way that chooses her needs above your comfort. Christ didn't dominate His Bride—He died for her. He didn't crush her flaws—He covered them with mercy.

That's your standard: not just to protect your wife, but to sacrifice for her.

Jesus: The Greatest Warrior Was a Servant

Everything about Jesus screams strength. He rebuked storms. He cast out demons. He walked through crowds trying to kill Him. He stood silent before accusation. He took every lash, every nail, and every insult with dignity and purpose.

But His greatest victory didn't come through control. It came through surrender.

> "No one takes My life from Me. I lay it down of My own accord." (John 10:18)

When Jesus laid down His life, He crushed the head of the serpent. And that act of divine love became the blueprint for every husband who wants to lead like Christ.

You don't war for her by overpowering her—you war for her by laying yourself down.

Sacrificial Love Is the Most Powerful Weapon

Your words might be sharp, your opinions well-reasoned, your logic airtight—but if they're not wrapped in sacrificial love, they will always fall short.

1 Corinthians 13 makes it clear:

> "If I have not love, I am nothing… love does not insist on its own way… love bears all things, believes all things, hopes all things, endures all things."

Sacrificial love chooses:

- Humility over pride
- Gentleness over dominance
- Forgiveness over retaliation
- Presence over escape

Sacrifice is not weakness. It's the strongest form of leadership you'll ever walk in.

Common Places Husbands Resist Sacrifice

1. Time
   - You say, "I'm working for my family," but never with your family.
   - Sacrificial love makes time, even when it's inconvenient.

2. Control
   - You want things done your way. But love lets go of the need to be right all the time.
   - Jesus washed feet. So should you.

3. Sexual purity
   ○ You want intimacy, but are you willing to guard your eyes, your phone, and your thoughts?
   ○ Sacrifice means killing secret sin for her emotional safety.

4. Emotional comfort
   ○ It's easier to shut down than to engage hard conversations.
   ○ Sacrificial love leans in when you'd rather check out.

Sacrifice Doesn't Always Feel Like Victory—But It Is

Sometimes, dying to yourself feels like losing:

- Apologizing first when you feel wronged
- Choosing silence when your pride wants to speak
- Serving without thanks
- Being patient with her healing process

But remember: the cross didn't look like victory either—until resurrection proved otherwise.

The enemy wants you to believe you're weak for choosing sacrificial love. But heaven sees it as warfare. Every time you deny your flesh to serve her, you break hell's grip on your home.

Practical Ways to Love Sacrificially

- Be interruptible.
  Put down your phone. Pause the game. Look her in the eyes.
- Affirm her often.
  Not just what she does—but who she is.
- Serve in small ways.
  Clean the kitchen. Run the errand. Speak peace in her stress.
- Pray over her when she least expects it.
  A whispered prayer at bedtime is louder than a thousand sermons.
- Protect her emotionally.
  Guard her heart like you would your own. Speak to her the way Christ speaks to you: with grace and truth.

Reflection Questions

- Am I more focused on being right than being loving?
- Where have I resisted laying myself down?
- What would it look like to love her like Jesus today?
- Is my leadership marked by control—or by compassion?

Devotional Prayer: Teach Me to Love Like You

Father,

I confess—I often love with conditions. I serve when it's convenient. I lead when it benefits me. But that's not the way of the cross. And it's not the way You loved me.

Teach me to love sacrificially.

Break my addiction to comfort, control, and pride.

Open my eyes to the ways I've wounded her through self-centeredness.

Make me a man who mirrors Jesus—not in word, but in action.

Give me the strength to die to myself.

Give me joy in service.

Give me grace in silence.

Give me courage to love her when she's tired, unsure, or hurting.

Jesus, You laid everything down for Your Bride.

Help me do the same.

In Your name,

Amen.

CHAPTER 5

The Sword of the Spirit

You cannot fight spiritual battles with emotional weapons.

You will never win a spiritual war with natural tools. Anger won't cast out fear. Logic won't silence lies. And your volume doesn't carry the power of victory—your voice in agreement with God's Word does.

God has equipped you with a weapon that never runs out of ammunition:

> "Take…the sword of the Spirit, which is the Word
> of God." (Ephesians 6:17)

This isn't metaphor—it's instruction. In the realm of spiritual warfare, there is only one offensive weapon: the Word. Everything else is armor to protect you. But the Word? It cuts. It drives out darkness. It silences deception. It reshapes atmospheres.

As a husband who wars for his wife, your greatest advantage is not your personality, your intellect, or even your experience—it's your ability to use Scripture like a sword.

Jesus: Wielding the Word in the Wilderness

When Satan confronted Jesus in the wilderness (Matthew 4:1–11), he didn't come with horns and fire—he came with words. Twisted truths. Emotional triggers. Scriptural distortion.

And Jesus didn't argue.

He didn't panic.

He didn't scream.

He said three words that every husband must learn to use:

"It is written."

Each temptation was met with Scripture. Not emotion. Not assumption. Not clever reasoning. But the spoken, living Word of God.

- "It is written: Man shall not live on bread alone..."
- "It is written: Worship the Lord your God and serve Him only..."
- "It is written: Do not put the Lord your God to the test..."

And the devil fled.

That's your model.

Your Home Needs a Husband Who Knows the Word

Satan is still whispering to your wife today:

- "You're not enough."
- "He's disappointed in you."
- "God doesn't hear you."
- "You'll always struggle with this."

If you don't speak the truth, the lie stays.

Your wife doesn't need shallow compliments or religious clichés. She needs a man who knows how to war in the Spirit—who sees the attack, grabs his sword, and cuts through the fog with clarity.

Why Many Husbands Feel Powerless

Some men love God but feel unequipped to fight spiritually. Why?

- They haven't been taught to read the Word as a weapon.
- They only open Scripture on Sundays.
- They depend on their wives to be the spiritual compass of the home.
- They know how to quote sports stats or business terms—but not one verse to break anxiety.

That stops now.

God isn't calling you to be a scholar. He's calling you to be dangerous to darkness.

How to Sharpen Your Sword

1. Read to Remember
   - Don't just read the Word to "check a box."
   - Read it like your family's peace depends on it—because it does.

2. Speak it Out Loud
   - The enemy doesn't fear your silence—he fears your declaration.
   - The Word of God spoken in faith turns your mouth into a weapon.

3. Pray It Over Her
   - Don't just pray from emotion—pray from revelation.
   - Example:
   - "God, You said You would keep her in perfect peace when her mind is stayed on You" (Isaiah 26:3).
   - "You said You would complete the good work You started in her" (Philippians 1:6).

4. Write It Around Your Home
   - Put Scripture on mirrors, walls, entryways.
   - Let your wife—and your children—see what your house is built on.

Scriptures to Use as a Sword for Your Wife

- Identity:
  "She is fearfully and wonderfully made." – Psalm 139:14
  "She is God's workmanship, created in Christ Jesus…" –
  Ephesians 2:10
- Peace:
  "You will keep her in perfect peace whose mind is stayed
  on You." – Isaiah 26:3
  "God has not given her a spirit of fear…" – 2 Timothy 1:7
- Strength:
  "She is clothed with strength and dignity…" – Proverbs
  31:25
  "The joy of the Lord is her strength." – Nehemiah 8:10
- Marriage unity:
  "What God has joined together, let no man separate." –
  Mark 10:9
  "A cord of three strands is not easily broken." –
  Ecclesiastes 4:12

Fighting Wrong: Emotional Weapons vs. the Word

Emotional Weapon	Temporary Result	Word of God Effect
Anger	Silence from your wife	Soft word brings peace (Proverbs 15:1)
Sarcasm	Shame or confusion	Grace-filled speech heals (Col. 4:6)
Withdrawal	Emotional distance	The Lord draws near (James 4:8)
Control	Fear and resentment	Perfect love casts out fear (1 John 4)

Don't confuse force with authority.

Don't settle for noise when you've been given a sword.

Reflection Questions

- Do I know God's Word well enough to use it in spiritual warfare?
- When was the last time I spoke Scripture over my wife out loud?
- Have I used emotional weapons more than spiritual ones?
- What verse will I memorize this week for my home?

▌ Devotional Prayer: Sharpen My Sword

Father,

I've too often fought in the flesh. I've raised my voice, but not my sword. I've used emotion, logic, and pride instead of standing on Your Word.

Teach me to love Your Word.

Give me a hunger to study it, speak it, and stand on it.

Make me a husband who doesn't just react—but one who wars with truth.

Let Your promises fill my mouth.

Let Your Spirit sharpen my discernment.

Let my prayers be filled with Scripture.

Let my leadership be rooted in Your voice.

I repent for every time I was silent when the enemy spoke.

From this day on, I will speak what is written.

I take up the Sword of the Spirit—

and I choose to fight the right enemy, with the right weapon, in the right spirit.

In Jesus' name,

Amen.

CHAPTER 6

Guarding Her Mind and Emotions

You are a watchman over her peace.

You protect what you value. Most men understand how to guard a house from physical threats. Deadbolts. Alarms. Security cameras. But few realize that their wife's mind and emotions are under far greater attack than the front door ever will be.

She is not just your partner. She is your responsibility. And while you're not her Savior, you are her spiritual watchman. You are called to be aware of what's threatening her peace, her thoughts, and her emotional health.

> "Above all else, guard your heart, for everything
> you do flows from it." (Proverbs 4:23)

You are called to guard the heart of the woman God entrusted to you—not through control, but through compassion; not with suspicion, but with Spirit-led discernment.

Elkanah and Hannah: A Picture of Emotional Discernment

In 1 Samuel 1, we meet Hannah—desperate for a child, emotionally drained, and constantly provoked by her rival. Her soul is in agony. And while her husband Elkanah doesn't fully understand her pain, he doesn't dismiss it either.

> "Her husband Elkanah said to her, 'Hannah, why are you weeping? Why don't you eat? Why are you downhearted?'" (1 Samuel 1:8)

He noticed her tears.

He spoke to her emotional state.

He pursued her heart even when she couldn't explain it.

That's what a husband does when he's emotionally alert. He leans in. He doesn't need a five-point explanation. He senses her burden. He covers her pain. He becomes a safe place.

The Emotional Landscape Your Wife Lives In

Many husbands don't realize what their wives silently carry:

- Insecurity – Am I beautiful to him? Am I enough? Does he see me?
- Shame – From past mistakes, from family wounds, from the feeling of failure
- Fear – About finances, her future, parenting, aging, or being emotionally abandoned
- Mental fatigue – From juggling roles, unspoken expectations, and spiritual attacks

These are not "overreactions." These are real battlegrounds in her mind—and they require more than patience. They require spiritual protection.

Your Role as Her Emotional Guard

You're not called to be a mind-reader. But you are called to be:

- Present – not just in body, but in attention
- Perceptive – noticing shifts in her tone, rhythm, or demeanor
- Prayerful – asking the Holy Spirit what's really going on under the surface
- Protective – speaking life and truth when lies or fear start speaking louder

A man of God doesn't wait until she collapses emotionally to step in. He notices the cracks and reinforces her with love, affirmation, and spiritual clarity.

Five Ways the Enemy Attacks Her Mind

1. Comparison
   - Social media, body image, unrealistic expectations

2. Condemnation
   - Whispering shame about past sins or current struggles

3. Isolation
   - Convincing her that no one understands what she's going through

4. Miscommunication
   - Twisting your tone, reinterpreting your silence as rejection

5. Discouragement
   - Draining her hope for breakthrough, healing, or restoration

Your Response as a Husband of War

1. Ask Questions That Open Her Heart
   - "What's been weighing on you lately?"
   - "How can I pray for you right now?"

      o   "Is there a lie you've been battling in your mind this week?"

2.   Be Tender in Timing
- o   Don't try to fix her in the middle of a breakdown. Hold her.
- o   Silence, tears, and stillness can be holy ground.

3.   Speak Truth Regularly
- o   Use Scripture to affirm her worth, purpose, beauty, and identity.

4.   Guard What Comes Into the Home
- o   Music. Shows. Conversations. Energy. If it doesn't protect her peace, it doesn't belong.

5.   Be a Consistent Voice of Calm
- o   You don't need all the right words. You just need to be a steady, safe place.

Sample Scriptures to Declare Over Her Mind

- "You have not been given a spirit of fear, but of power, love, and a sound mind." (2 Timothy 1:7)
- "The peace of God, which surpasses all understanding, will guard your heart and your mind." (Philippians 4:7)
- "You are God's masterpiece, created in Christ Jesus to do good works." (Ephesians 2:10)
- "The joy of the Lord is your strength." (Nehemiah 8:10)

Don't just think these verses. Speak them. Declare them. Live them.

Reflection Questions

- Am I emotionally present for my wife, or distracted by stress and routine?
- Do I notice when her countenance changes—or do I overlook it?
- What lie has she been fighting, and how can I replace it with truth?
- Have I invited the Holy Spirit to help me be a better emotional protector?

Devotional Prayer: Make Me a Safe Place

Father,

Make me a shelter for her mind. A refuge for her soul. A place where she can exhale and feel covered—not just physically, but emotionally. Give me discernment to see what she cannot say. Give me courage to speak peace when she feels chaos. Give me wisdom to guard our home with tenderness and spiritual strength.

Let my arms be safe.

Let my tone bring calm.

Let my words bring healing.

Let my leadership reflect Your kindness.

I reject passivity and distraction.

I will not let the enemy torment her without resistance.

I declare peace over her mind, strength in her heart, and clarity in her spirit.

Make me a husband who protects her not just with hands—but with heart.

In Jesus' name,

Amen.

CHAPTER 7

Warring as One

There is no power like a unified marriage in Christ.

Some of the most dangerous words in a marriage are:

"We're just not on the same page."

Disconnection doesn't always happen with shouting or betrayal. Often, it creeps in silently—through busy schedules, unspoken frustrations, and slowly drifting priorities. And when a husband and wife stop fighting together, they start fighting alone.

Satan knows this. That's why his first strategy isn't full assault—it's quiet division. If he can fracture your agreement, he can diminish your authority.

But when a husband and wife walk in spiritual unity, their marriage becomes a force that shakes darkness and births Kingdom fruit.

"If two of you agree here on earth concerning anything you ask, my Father in heaven will do it for you." (Matthew 18:19)

Agreement is spiritual power. Unity is spiritual warfare. And when you war as one, God fights with you.

Aquila and Priscilla: A Kingdom Couple in Sync

Acts 18 introduces us to a married couple who quietly played a vital role in the early church: Aquila and Priscilla. They were:

- Tentmakers by trade
- Teachers of the Word
- Partners in ministry
- Hosts to the Apostle Paul
- Disciplers of Apollos, one of the most powerful preachers of the time

They weren't just married—they were in mission.

You don't read about Aquila arguing while Priscilla preached. You don't see one of them outpacing the other spiritually. They moved in harmony. Their marriage was a platform for God's power.

You were never called to build your own legacy. You were called to build something eternal—together.

What It Means to "War as One"

1.

Spiritual Agreement

- Praying the same things.
- Believing the same promises.
- Declaring the same Word.

When you pray together in unity, your authority multiplies.

2.

Emotional Alignment

- Fighting for connection, not control.
- Learning each other's emotional rhythms and honoring them.

Love without unity is fragile. Unity without communication is fake.

3.

Purposeful Partnership

- Asking, "What has God called us to build, give, and do together?"
- Every couple has a shared assignment. Find it—and fight for it.

Enemies of Unity

1. Pride
   - "I have to win this argument."
   - Unity loses when ego wins.

2. Unspoken Expectations
   - "You should have known I needed support."
   - Unexpressed needs create resentment.

3. Busyness
   - Full calendars. Empty hearts.
   - Intimacy doesn't survive on leftovers.

4. Lack of Prayer Together
   - No spiritual unity leads to confusion and defensiveness.

Signs You're Not Warring as One

- You pray individually, but never together.
- Conflict lingers without resolution.
- You avoid spiritual conversations.
- You feel emotionally alone, even when physically together.

These are not symptoms to ignore—they're signals to act.

How to Rebuild Unity

1. Start Small with Prayer
   - Just 1–2 minutes a day.
   - Even "God, thank You for today. Protect our hearts" is powerful.

2. Choose One Purpose to Pursue Together
   - Serve somewhere. Give something. Believe for something as one.

3. Do a Spiritual Check-In Weekly
   - Ask: "Where do you feel spiritually dry? What's bringing you life? What are you battling in your heart right now?"

4. Fast Together for a Breakthrough
   - Agree to deny something physical to fight for something spiritual.

5. Worship Together
   - At church. In the car. In the kitchen.
   - Nothing aligns hearts like joint adoration of the same King.

Declaration of Oneness

"What God has joined together, let no one separate." (Mark 10:9)

That's not just a wedding verse. That's a war cry. No one—no lie, no sin, no pattern, no generational curse—has the right to separate what God united.

So guard your unity.

Fight for your agreement.

Speak peace over your connection.

When you war as one, you not only protect your marriage—you advance the Kingdom.

Reflection Questions

- Are we praying together regularly—or just surviving together?
- Do we have a shared sense of purpose in this season?
- What spiritual attacks are trying to divide our unity?
- What's one step we can take this week to war as one?

Devotional Prayer: Make Us One Again

Father,

Forgive me for letting our unity slip. Forgive me for the silent distance, the unspoken offenses, the spiritual apathy. I want more than just a peaceful home—I want a unified one. A powerful one. A marriage that moves heaven and stops hell.

Teach us to pray together.

Teach us to dream together.

Teach us to serve together.

Bind our hearts with cords that cannot be broken.

Break every scheme of the enemy that would divide us.

Silence every lie that would pit us against one another.

Restore what pride, pain, or pressure has weakened.

Make our marriage a threat to darkness.

Make our love a testimony of Your grace.

Make us one again.

In Jesus' name,

Amen.

CHAPTER 8

Raising the Standard in the Home

> **The war is won when your home becomes a fortress of faith.**

You don't drift into a godly home. You build it.

Brick by brick. Prayer by prayer. Choice by choice.

As a husband, you are not just a provider or protector—you are a standard-bearer. You set the spiritual atmosphere of your home. You create the tone, the temperature, and the level of spiritual hunger in your household.

> "As for me and my house, we will serve the Lord."
> (Joshua 24:15)

This was not a casual statement. It was a line drawn in the sand. Joshua was surrounded by idol worship, cultural compromise, and wavering commitment. But he didn't ask his household for a vote. He made a declaration.

He didn't say, "We'll try our best."

He said, "We will serve the Lord."

That's the kind of bold, non-negotiable leadership today's homes desperately need.

Joshua: The Standard-Setter

Joshua had seen what happens when people live without conviction. He saw a generation wander in circles because they feared giants more than they trusted God. He saw how low the standard could fall when leaders stayed silent.

So when he reached the end of his life, he stood before the nation and said what every godly husband must learn to say:

> "You choose who you'll serve, but as for me and
> my house…"

He took ownership. He led with conviction. And that standard didn't just impact his tent—it impacted generations.

That's what godly standards do: they outlive you.

What Is a "Standard" in the Home?

A standard is a spiritual expectation anchored in God's Word. It's a line that says:

- This is what we believe.
- This is how we speak.
- This is what we allow—and what we don't.

You can't control everything your family experiences outside your house, but you can absolutely set the standard inside of it.

Common Areas Where the Standard Must Be Set

1. Speech
   - No dishonor, sarcasm, or emotional violence.
   - Words must build, not break.

2. Entertainment
   - What are you watching together? Listening to? Laughing at?
   - If it grieves the Holy Spirit, it doesn't belong in your living room.

3. Time With God
   - Is Scripture read? Is prayer a rhythm or a last resort?
   - Make spiritual habits non-negotiable, not optional.

4. Conflict Resolution
    o   You don't go to sleep in division.
    o   You speak truth in love, not silence in pride.

5. Honor and Holiness
    o   How do you talk about others?
    o   How is sin handled? With tolerance—or with truth and grace?

How Standards Get Lowered

- Passivity: "It's not a big deal."
- Busyness: "We just don't have time for devotionals anymore."
- Culture Creep: "Everyone else watches this."
- People-Pleasing: "Let's not make the kids feel uncomfortable."
- Avoiding Conflict: "If I bring that up, she'll get upset."

But here's the truth: what you allow repeatedly becomes your new normal.

If you don't set the standard, the world will.

Raising the Standard Means:

1. Leading in Repentance
    o   Not waiting for others to "get right," but modeling it daily.

55

- A godly home is led by a husband who says, "I was wrong—please forgive me."

2. Declaring What's Allowed
   - Out loud. With love. With conviction.
   - "In this house, we don't gossip."
   - "In this home, we forgive quickly."
   - "In this family, we seek God first."

3. Rebuilding When You've Let Things Slide
   - You don't need to feel ashamed—you just need to course-correct.
   - Reset the tone today.

4. Blessing Your Home Verbally
   - Speak God's Word over every room.
   - Anoint the doorposts.
   - Pray aloud before meals, bedtime, and moments of stress.

Establishing a Fortress of Faith

You want your home to be more than peaceful—you want it to be a place where heaven feels welcome and hell feels unwelcome.

That means:

- Prayer isn't awkward. It's normal.
- Worship isn't reserved for Sundays. It happens during dishes.

- Apologies aren't delayed. They're initiated quickly.
- God's presence isn't a guest. He's the owner.

When you raise the standard, you don't just protect your family—you shape the future.

Reflection Questions

- What spiritual standards have I neglected in my home?
- Where have I allowed culture to creep into our values or habits?
- Have I made the spiritual tone of our home clear—and consistent?
- What one standard can I reestablish this week?

Devotional Prayer: Let My Home Be Yours

Father,

Thank You for entrusting me with this home. I surrender every room, every rhythm, every moment to You. Forgive me for the moments I've tolerated things that compromise Your presence. Forgive me for lowering the standard to avoid conflict or keep the peace.

I declare that my home belongs to You.

My marriage will reflect Your covenant.

My children will know Your name.

My walls will echo with truth and peace.

Help me lead not with control, but with conviction.

Let my love be strong, but gentle.

Let my decisions reflect eternity.

Let my home be a place where darkness cannot hide, and where Your Spirit dwells richly.

Make me a standard-bearer.

Make this home a fortress of faith.

In Jesus' name,

Amen.

Born to War, Called to Love

This is more than a marriage book—it's a call to battle.

You've read every chapter. You've been challenged to pray, to lead, to serve, to repent, and to war for the heart of your wife. But before you put this book down, I need you to understand something:

You were never meant to be a passive man.

You were never created to sit on the sidelines while your marriage suffered silently.

You were never designed to let the world disciple your wife while you remained spiritually silent.

You were never supposed to inherit a calling and leave it unused.

You were called to be a warrior—not just in theory, but in practice.

And not just any warrior. A husband-warrior.

One who doesn't just win arguments, but wins her trust.

One who doesn't just provide income, but provides intercession.

One who doesn't just protect the house, but fights for holiness inside it.

One who doesn't just quote Scripture—but lives it, bleeds for it, and covers his wife with it.

▌ Let This Be the Day You Drew a Line

Maybe you've spent years asleep in your calling. Maybe you didn't know how to lead. Maybe you thought your wife was the "spiritual one." Maybe you've failed more times than you can count.

Here's the good news:

God doesn't call perfect husbands.

He calls surrendered ones.

David was a murderer and adulterer.

Peter denied Jesus three times.

Moses killed a man.

Yet all of them became weapons in the hands of God—because they repented and followed Him.

So draw your line in the sand today:

As for me and my house, we will serve the Lord.

As for me and my marriage, I will no longer fight her—I will fight for her.

As for me and my identity, I will no longer be passive—I will walk in my calling as a priest, protector, and pursuer.

The War Is Real, But the Victory Is Ours

Let's be clear: Satan won't roll over just because you read a book.

He will test your decision.

He will whisper lies.

He will push back when you start raising the standard.

But you're not fighting for victory—you're fighting from it.

Jesus already crushed the head of the serpent.

He already gave you the armor.

He already gave you the Spirit.

He already gave you authority in His name.

So don't back down.

Don't fall asleep again.

Don't go silent.

Your wife needs your voice.

Your children need your leadership.

Your home needs your conviction.

The world needs your example.

You Are the Gatekeeper Now

You're the thermostat, not the thermometer. You don't just reflect the temperature—you set it.

You're the first to repent.

The first to pray.

The first to serve.

The first to speak peace when chaos rises.

You don't wait to be asked.

You don't lead only when she agrees.

You lead when it's hard. When it's costly. When it's lonely.

That's what love does. That's what a man of war does.

And One Day...

You will stand before God—not just as a man, but as a husband.

And He won't ask how successful you were in business.

He won't ask how many followers you had.

He won't ask if you won every debate.

He'll ask:

- Did you cover her?
- Did you intercede?
- Did you serve her like My Son served the Church?
- Did you war for her in the Spirit?

Let the answer be "Yes, Lord. I didn't lead perfectly, but I led faithfully."

This Is the Call:

- To pick up your sword—the Word of God
- To pick up your towel—like Jesus washing feet
- To pick up your cross—and die daily to your pride
- To pick up your post—as the guardian of your home

This is not the end of a book. This is the beginning of a new legacy.

You are a husband who wars.

You are a man of the Word.

You are a leader of love.

You are a fighter who finishes well.

Let the war begin—and let love win.

Devotional Prayer: The Final Surrender

Father,

I answer the call. I will not be passive. I will not be quiet. I will not let fear keep me from leading. Make me a man of war—bold in truth, broken in pride, steady in love.

I surrender every area where I've been silent.

I lay down every excuse I've used to avoid responsibility.

I repent for the times I wounded with words or withheld affection.

Teach me how to fight with wisdom.

Teach me how to love with endurance.

Teach me how to lead with humility.

Teach me how to listen to Your Spirit in the middle of battle.

Let my marriage reflect the gospel.

Let my leadership reflect the cross.

Let my house be a place where darkness trembles and heaven dwells.

I am Yours.

She is Yours.

This marriage is Yours.

And I will war until my last breath to reflect Your glory.

In Jesus' name,

Amen.